Salt-N-Pepa

Sahara Gisnash

The Rosen Publishing Group, Inc., New York

To Melissa Jaeger-Miller

Published in 2006 by The Rosen Publishing Group, Inc.
29 East 21st Street, New York, NY 10010

First Edition

Library of Congress Cataloging-in-Publication Data

Gisnash, Sahara.
Salt-n-Pepa/by Sahara Gisnash. — 1st ed.
    p. cm. — (The library of hip-hop biographies)
Includes bibliographical references (p.), discography (p.), and index.
ISBN 1-4042-0520-9 (library binding)
1. Salt-n-Pepa (Musical group) 2. Rap musicians — United States —
Biography. I. Title. II. Series.
ML421.S235G57 2006
782.421649'092'2–dc22

2005021598

Manufactured in the United States of America

On the cover: A group photograph of Salt-N-Pepa.

CONTENTS

INTRODUCTION

Salt-N-Pepa is the most successful all-female hip-hop group of all time. The group is outspoken, strong, and independent. Its songs are playful, intelligent, and always pro-woman in the sense that they challenge many of the negative portrayals of women that have been common in hip-hop. Ever since its debut in 1985, Salt-N-Pepa has proved that hip-hop isn't just a man's world.

Salt-N-Pepa started out in hip-hop's early days with a raw sound, hot moves, and bad-girl attitude. Over the years, its members have grown and its style has become more sophisticated. Today, the group has a Grammy, several platinum albums, and fans all over the world. But perhaps most important, the ladies of Salt-N-Pepa discovered that they have a message they want the world to hear: believe in yourself, respect others, and make the world a better place.

It's a message that comes straight from the group's own experiences. Salt-N-Pepa started out as front women who performed music written and produced by others. After breaking away from their domineering manager/producer, the trio began writing and producing its own material. This new creative control led the group to greater success, as fans around the world responded to its spirited songs with feminist messages and danceable beats. The members of the group learned how to manage their money and began to take care of their own business affairs. They became mothers and took up causes such as raising awareness about low-birth-weight babies and AIDS education. Salt-N-Pepa is living proof that with hard work and determination, anything is possible.

CHAPTER ONE

GIRLS NEXT DOOR

The members of Salt-N-Pepa grew up in New York City during the 1970s and early 1980s. Growing up during hip–hop's early years was important to the trio's development into the genre's first megastar girl group.

Salt was born Cheryl James in Brooklyn, New York, on March 28, 1969. She grew up in Queens, a borough of New York City, with her parents, an older brother, and a younger sister. Her first time performing for an audience was in a church play at age nine. She played a rhyming witch. Cheryl eventually grew into a serious, introspective young woman. In many ways, she was the opposite of Pepa.

Pepa was born Sandra Denton on November 9, 1969, in Kingston, Jamaica. She and her family moved to Queens when she was just a little girl. Sandy (as her friends call her) came from a large family. She had seven sisters and one brother. Even as a little girl, she loved being the center of attention, playing rock star by using a broomstick as a make-believe microphone. However, Sandy also remembers getting teased and suffering from low self-esteem. Nevertheless, she grew up to be a loud, fun-loving punk rocker who always had a lot of friends.

The third member of the group was the DJ known as Spinderella. Two women would fill this role. The first was Pamela Latoya Greene, who was later replaced by Deirdre Roper.

HIP-HOP EXPLOSION!

Hip-hop was born in the late 1970s in the South Bronx, a very poor New York City neighborhood filled with abandoned buildings and vacant lots. This bleak world, then mostly associated with drugs, violence, and disaffected youths, was the perfect breeding ground for a vibrant new youth culture celebrating self-expression.

Dissatisfied with what they considered bland music on the radio, young DJs began digging up old soul records and skipping straight to the break, or the funkiest part of the record. As

The members of Salt-N-Pepa were clearly b-girls before they became megastars. Throughout the group's career, the trio's raps, postures, attire, and attitude reflected those of the greater female hip-hop community. As they became more successful, they became trendsetters for their core audience.

DJs raced to piece together the funkiest series of songs, they invented scratching, looping, and other tricks.

Suddenly, the new sound was everywhere—at house parties, parks, local clubs, and high school dances. New, exciting dances followed, eventually evolving into break dancing. At the same time, artistic kids had started painting graffiti murals on subway trains and abandoned buildings. These cultural elements—break dancing, graffiti, and DJing—became three of the four pillars of hip-hop culture. The term "hip-hop" hadn't been coined yet; break-dancers and other devotees of the new sound called themselves b-boys and girls. The "b" stood for the breaks, the most important sonic element of the new sound. The new music slowly spread from the Bronx to Manhattan, Queens, Brooklyn, and New Jersey.

It wasn't until a little later that the MC, or rapper—the fourth pillar—stepped into the limelight. Originally, MCs did little more than give "shout outs" to friends in the audience and get the crowd excited. Eventually, it became clear that some people were better at getting a party started than others. Soon, MCs began to add rhymes to their repertoires, making up clever things to say. Little rhymes became freestyles, freestyles became written-out verses, verses became songs, and songs became group routines. Suddenly, MCs were almost as popular as DJs and had become the focus of hip-hop shows. MC crews such as the Fantastic Five choreographed dance routines and wore outrageous outfits at their concerts.

Most of the DJs during these very first days of hip-hop were men, such as Kool Herc, the godfather of DJing; Afrika Bambaataa, who played the widest variety of music at his parties; and Grandmaster Flash, who invented looping. Some important early MC crews were the Furious Five and the Cold Crush Brothers. Sha Rock, a female MC and member of the famed group Funky Four Plus One, was one of the most respected rappers on the early hip-hop scene. The Mercedes Ladies were the first all-female MC crew.

Then, in 1979, all the rules changed. Sugar Hill Records recorded a song entitled "Rapper's Delight" by a previously unknown group called the Sugar Hill Gang. It was one of the first commercially recorded rap songs, and it became the first true hip-hop hit. When the song hit the airwaves, it was so popular that New York City radio stations had to ask listeners not to call in and request it.

Hip-hop was on its way to becoming big business. For the first time, people realized that there might actually be a lot of money to be made in rap music. It had spread beyond the streets of New York City and was gaining popularity nationwide. Movies such as *Wild Style* (1982) and *Krush Groove* (1985) further spread the genre's appeal. When Queens natives Run DMC came out in 1983, hip-hop was ready to explode into the big time. With their street-tough style and more electronic sound, Run DMC's members became hip-hop's first superstars.

A CREW IS BORN

In this world bursting with creative energy, Salt and Pepa both were attending nursing school at Queensborough Community College. Pepa was the outrageous one. She had lots of friends, bleached-blond hair, and a wardrobe full of punk-rock clothes. She was daring and adventurous. Salt was quieter and more reserved. Together, they loved to roller-skate and have a good time.

Salt and Pepa were "discovered" in an unlikely place: a Sears telephone representative office. Salt helped Pepa get a part-time job calling Sears customers who had just bought appliances. As it turned out, this wasn't just any office. The ladies worked alongside Martin Lawrence, who would later become a world-renowned comedian, and Christopher Reid and Christopher Martin, who would later form Kid 'N Play, another very famous rap group.

Another one of their coworkers was an ambitious young man named Hurby "Luv Bug" Azor. Azor had belonged

This screen shot from the 1990 movie *House Party* shows Christopher "Play" Martin of Kid 'N Play and Martin Lawrence in their roles as hip-hopping party teenagers. The successful movie spawned two sequels.

to a rap group named the Super Loves, and he was taking a music producing class at New York City's Center for Media Arts. He asked Salt and Pepa to add vocals to a track he was recording for class. The song he wrote for them was called "The Showstopper (Is Stupid Fresh)." It was a response song to rapper Doug E. Fresh's hit song "The Show." In "The Show" and the song "La di da di," Doug E. Fresh and his partner, Slick Rick, describe being pursued by women whom they gleefully reject:

KID 'N PLAY

Salt-N-Pepa wasn't the only superstar rap group to be discovered by budding producer Hurby "Luv Bug" Azor. Christopher Reid and Christopher Martin were already MCs when they met Azor. In fact, Christopher Martin used to be in Azor's band, the Super Loves. Together, the three men created the sound and image of Kid 'N Play, which became one of the most commercially successful hip-hop groups of the era. Most people today remember Kid (Reid) as the sincere-looking rapper with the high-top, "eraser head" fade haircut. Play (Martin) was the smooth talker who always got the ladies. Together, they had a clean-cut image and a popular dance step—the Kid 'N Play, a modified version of an old jazz-age dance called the Charleston. The duo also had a very successful career in movies. Their hit movie *House Party* (1990) earned them two sequels and another movie called *Class Act* (1992). The group also had a short-lived Saturday morning cartoon series, *Kid 'N Play*.

Slick Rick: Stepped on the D-train at 205th
I saw a pretty girl
Doug E. Fresh: So?
Slick Rick: So I sat beside her
Then she went "ROAR!" like she was Tony the Tiger
I said, oh no, there's been a mistake
Honey, my name's Slick Rick not Frosted Flakes!

"The Showstopper" told the story from a woman's perspective. It made fun of Doug E. Fresh and Slick Rick for being so full of themselves:

> *Salt: The train made a stop*
> *Pepa: Where?*
> *Salt: Two hundred and five*
> *And a little soft guy walked inside*
> *He wore plastic Bally's and a booty Gucci suit*
> *Cracked a little smile and showed a fake gold tooth*
> *Pepa: Was he cute?*
> *Salt: Negative, he was a dupe.*

Roxanne Shante, whose real name is Lolita Shante Gooden, became somewhat of a hip-hop legend because of her groundbreaking response song "Roxanne's Revenge." Although she enjoyed a couple of other hits in the two years following the release of "Roxanne's Revenge," she was never able to parlay the buzz surrounding that hit into a successful rap career. She is pictured here in 2004 at the third annual H20 Film Festival Odyssey Awards in New York City.

Azor wasn't the first one to come up with the idea of a response record. Just the year before, male group UTFO's hit song "Roxanne," about a stuck-up girl who ignores men's advances, had inspired a slew of response records. The first, and most famous, came from a fourteen-year-old girl who called herself Roxanne Shante. Her song, "Roxanne's

HIP-HOP RESPONSE SONGS

A response song is a song that responds to a hit by another artist. Sometimes a response song is an answer to a musical challenge. Hip-hop is full of musical feuds. But there is a special tradition of women rappers responding to offensive songs by male rappers, and vice versa. For instance, when female rappers TLC recorded "No Scrubs," criticizing men without any money, male group Sporty Thieves responded with a song called "No Pigeons," which put down stuck-up women. Response records continue to be a popular feature of hip-hop culture today.

Revenge," told the girl's side of the story. It was tough and funky, and it became a big hit. Twenty-five thousand copies of the single were sold in New York City alone. Soon, other groups were releasing their own responses to "Roxanne," with titles such as "Roxanne, You're Through," "Roxanne's a Man," and "Roxanne's Mother." Legend has it that the storm of response records didn't stop until more than 100 "Roxanne" songs had been recorded! Azor knew that recording a response to a popular song like "The Show" would be a smart business move.

Everyone liked "The Showstopper" so much that Azor played it for local radio DJ Marley Marl, who agreed to air it on his show. Azor hadn't dreamed up the name Salt-N-Pepa yet; the single debuted under the name Supernature. It became an underground success. Salt told hip-hop writer and DJ Davey D, "This little record company called Pop Arts Records wrote us and asked us if we wanted to put it on wax. Then we quit school, our jobs and we was doing the club circuit, and then after that we just kept going." Azor decided to round out the group with a female DJ, Pamela Latoya Greene, who took the name Spinderella. The group became Salt-N-Pepa, after a line in "The Showstoppers." The women were known for putting on a great stage show, choreographing their own dance routines, getting the audience involved, and having a lot of fun.

The ladies had hard work to do in these early days. In the book *Working Musicians*, Salt remembers, "I've never worked harder in my career than when Salt-N-Pepa first started. I would do anything. I would sleep in the studio and wake up in the studio. Nothing mattered. I would spend my last little part-time job check in the studio and just drive to any function. Nothing was too far for a little club date." That hard work was about to pay off. The success of Salt-N-Pepa's single on Pop Arts Records led to a record deal on Next Plateau Records. Salt-N-Pepa recorded its first full-length album, *Hot, Cool, and Vicious*, in 1986.

CHAPTER TWO

SUCCESS

Hot, Cool, and Vicious was a genuine hit. It was filled with stylish rhymes and sexy songs with bad-girl attitude. On the funky "I'll Take Your Man," the ladies issued a challenge to all women who might stand in their way: "Don't ya know / Can't ya understand / Mess with me / and I'll take your man!" "My Mic Sounds Nice" was a classic boasting track that focused on the ladies' skills as MCs. Azor pointed out that the song could have easily been rapped by a man (meaning that, at a time when hip-hop was widely considered to be a guy

Salt-N-Pepa's early success made the trio a priority at its record company and brought such benefits as professional stylists, who gave the group a more polished look. Yet the group never lost its street credibility, because its edge and around-the-way-girl attitude are always prominent in its work.

thing, the lyrics and rapping were solid enough to be considered authentic).

But it was "Push It," a song that the group claims it recorded as a joke, that really brought Salt-N-Pepa to the world's attention. The song was raw, outspoken, and very danceable. The video featured Salt-N-Pepa in the latest fly (fashionable) gear, performing for an enthusiastic crowd, rapping and dancing provocatively. The single sold more than a million copies, soared to the top of the R & B charts, and earned the group its first Grammy nomination. However, Salt-N-Pepa boycotted the awards ceremony after learning that the hip-hop category would not be televised. *Hot, Cool, and Vicious* became the first album by a female rap group to go double platinum.

SPINDERELLA'S NOT A FELLA, SHE'S A GIRL DJ

Hip-hop music had truly started with the DJ, and early rap music was much more centered around the DJ than it is today. The DJ was the one who made the party happen by playing the "hypest" songs and getting the crowd dancing. The DJ was the heart of any hip-hop group.

Azor knew it was important for his new all-female act to have a DJ. He envisioned Salt-N-Pepa as having two rappers, Salt and Pepa, and a DJ, Spinderella. The first Spinderella was Pamela Latoya Greene. In fact, she went on to have a minor solo career as the Original Spinderella. In 1987, sixteen-year-old Deirdre Roper (Dee Dee to her friends) replaced Greene as the group's personal female DJ.

Roper grew up with her three sisters and two brothers in the Louis H. Pink Houses in East New York, Brooklyn. She was the second youngest in her family, and her protective parents were strict with her. The projects where she lived were rough, but they didn't stifle her creativity. She learned how to DJ from a boyfriend at Franklin K. Lane High School.

After the launch of *Hot, Cool, and Vicious*, Azor asked Roper to become the group's new Spinderella. Roper was excited by the idea, but first she had to get permission from her skeptical parents. Salt, Pepa, Azor, and their friend—identified only as J. P.—(then Azor's comanager) all pitched in to win the Roper family over. In the book *Hip Hop Divas*, Spinderella told writer Harry Allen, "J. P. was real instrumental at that point because he knew what my parents were feeling. He talked about curfew; he spoke about schooling. Then Cheryl [Salt] was like, 'When we go on the road, she'll stay in my room, I'll take care of her, and I'll make sure she won't get into any trouble.' They all spoke on my behalf. And then my family had to look at that like, 'Wow, this is bigger than we thought.'" Finally, Roper's mother caved in, and the young DJ was allowed to join Salt-N-Pepa. She made her debut as Spinderella in the video for "Push It." She would be with Salt-N-Pepa for the next decade and a half.

A SALT WITH A DEADLY PEPA

Azor was anxious to capitalize on the success of *Hot, Cool, and Vicious* with a fresh collection of hits, so he rushed the trio into the studio to record *A Salt with a Deadly Pepa*. The 1988 album sold well. However, it disappointed critics, who felt the new material wasn't very good. Many people said that the album felt rushed

Fans of Salt-N-Pepa could rely on the trio releasing vibrant music videos to its hit singles. The three members were great dancers who were always ready to put on a good show. Salt-N-Pepa has been nominated for several MTV Music Video Awards, winning three for best dance video, best R & B video, and best choreography in 1994 for "Whatta Man."

and complained that the group hadn't taken enough time to make quality songs. Listeners were especially disappointed with "Twist and Shout," a reworking of the Isley Brothers' original 1962 hit.

But there was one innovative hit on the album, "Shake Your Thang," which fused hip-hop with a regional Washington, D.C., music style named go-go. The story goes that Salt-N-Pepa played a show in D.C. The group's opening act was local go-go band

WHAT IS GO-GO?

Around the same time that hip-hop was exploding in New York City, a new regional style was being born in Washington, D.C. Go-go was funk-based dance music that flourished in the 1980s in the U.S. capital. Like early hip-hop, it was party music meant to get a crowd rocking. Like hip-hop, it featured lots of call-and-response between the performers and the audience. Unlike hip-hop, go-go music was made exclusively by live bands, usually with guitar, lots of percussion, keyboards, and horns. Devotees of go-go saw the music as a return to the raw funk of James Brown in an era when too much music seemed soulless and electronic. For a while, some thought that go-go might spread across the United States and rival hip-hop for national popularity. But go-go never truly grew beyond D.C.'s borders. Today, it remains an underground regional style.

E.U. When Salt-N-Pepa's turntables broke down in the middle of its set, E.U. stepped in to help the group finish its songs. The merging of their two styles worked so well together that they decided to collaborate on an update of the Isley Brothers' 1969 hit tune "It's Your Thing." The resulting song, "Shake Your Thang," featured the lyric "I like my hip-hop mixed with go-go, baby. It's my thang and I shake it like crazy!"

Despite this innovation, the rest of the hip-hop world wondered if Salt-N-Pepa was intentionally blunting its edge to gain a wider audience. It was commercially successful, but could it continue to be innovative?

TENSION BEHIND THE SCENES

Salt and Azor had become an item, a true hip-hop power couple. She was one of hip-hop's greatest stars, and he was managing and producing both Salt-N-Pepa and Kid 'N Play, whose albums and movies were bringing hip-hop to a wider audience. Salt told writer Harry Allen, "I was very much in love with Hurby [Azor]. He was the first person I ever loved, and I've never loved anybody since like I loved Hurby."

However, this relationship caused some tension within the group. At the time, Azor totally controlled Salt-N-Pepa. He produced the group's music and coordinated its members' wardrobes. He even insisted that they follow his advice about how to act and whom to talk to. Since Salt was going out with Hurby, she supported him and his ideas. However, Pepa didn't like the idea of someone telling her what to do. Sometimes Pepa felt like her best friend was on someone else's side. A storm was on the horizon.

CHAPTER THREE

TRANSFORMATION, TRIAL, AND TRIUMPH

In the late 1980s and early 1990s, the music industry finally realized that hip-hop was more than just a passing fad. Fans around the country were discovering the new genre for the first time. Artists including MC Hammer and Vanilla Ice were becoming the first major "cross-over" acts, appealing to audiences across white America and the world with their pop-flavored songs. Young rapper Will Smith (of the duo DJ Jazzy Jeff and the Fresh Prince) starred in his own hit sitcom, *The Fresh Prince of Bel-Air*, in which he played an edgy but lovable hip-hop kid growing up with rich relatives. The show was a hit and made hip-hop culture even more acceptable to mainstream audiences. A major new talk show, *The Arsenio Hall Show*, with a hip-hop style and featuring a black host, debuted in 1990. Perhaps most important, the music television channel MTV finally debuted its first rap show, *Yo! MTV Raps*, in 1989.

At the same time, less mainstream hip-hop was changing and evolving. As hip-hop spread across the country, new regional styles were developing. The "old school" was being replaced by a variety of new styles and genres. "New jack swing" melded rap with R & B sounds, bringing designer clothes and smooth, clean looks to the forefront of hip-hop culture. In Los Angeles, California, gangsta rap was emerging, pairing funky beats from the 1970s with dark tales of inner-city violence and crime. Gangsta rap supergroup NWA was the first to make a splash in this new style in 1988. Meanwhile, the Native Tongues Posse, a loose group of MC crews, including the Jungle Brothers, A Tribe Called Quest, and De La Soul, took hip-hop in the opposite direction from gangsta rap, creating playful lyrics and jazzy hooks.

There was also a new surge in conscious rap that promoted social responsibility and political engagement. Wildly successful rap group Public Enemy challenged the status quo with its raps about black empowerment, urging its listeners to "fight the powers that be." Queen Latifah's raps were both feminist and Afrocentric. Her lyrics, which often claimed a certain regality for herself and among black women, and crownlike African headgear made her

Cohosts Ed Lover (*left*) and Dr. Dre (*right*) clown around with *Yo! MTV Raps* producer Ted Demme at the MTV Studios in New York in 1988. In an age when music videos became increasingly important in the marketing of popular music, *Yo! MTV Raps* helped raise the profile of hip-hop artists on the national stage.

a true hip-hop queen. Across the country, there was a growing sense that the new hip-hop nation should work together to achieve social change and real justice.

BLACKS' MAGIC

Meanwhile, Salt-N-Pepa was hard at work in the studio, creating a new album. Seeing that Azor was torn between managing the booming careers of Salt-N-Pepa and Kid 'N Play, Salt decided to take on some of the writing and producing for *Blacks' Magic* (1990). She had always been a socially conscious person, and now she began putting her ideas about the world around her—especially the battle of the sexes—into her songs. She wrote lyrics for the songs "Expression" and "Independent." The result was better, more intelligent songs, with deeper social messages.

Salt-N-Pepa had always rapped about female power. Now this came to the fore in hits such as "Expression," "Do You Want Me," and "Let's Talk About Sex," which spoke frankly about the need for women to be strong and independent. *Blacks' Magic* became the group's most successful album yet, with hits climbing not only the R & B charts but also the national pop charts. "Let's Talk About Sex," in particular, was a wildly successful single.

GIVING BACK

"Let's Talk About Sex" also became an anthem for safe sex at a time when the media was discovering the AIDS crisis. News anchor Peter Jennings asked Salt-N-Pepa to rerecord the song as "Let's Talk About AIDS" and based an ABC special called *In a New Light* around it. The video for "Let's Talk About AIDS" became a public service announcement in New York State. All proceeds from the song and video went to the National Minority AIDS Council and the TJ Martell Foundation for AIDS Research. In the song, Salt-N-Pepa rapped:

Spinderella, Salt, and Pepa *(from left to right)* lay down the vocals in the studio for a track on their *Blacks' Magic* album. With greater creative control, the trio produced a frank album that urged women to assert their strength and independence.

Don't dismiss, dis, or blacklist the topic
that ain't gonna stop it.
Now if you go about it right you just might save your life
don't be uptight, come join the fight.

Later on, Salt-N-Pepa stayed involved in the fight against AIDS and also raised awareness of other important issues such

THE AIDS CRISIS DURING THE 1980S

The deadly disease AIDS, or acquired immunodeficiency syndrome, first appeared in the United States in the early 1980s. At first, the disease was a mystery; all people knew was that it seemed to show up in otherwise healthy homosexual men, and it was deadly. For many years, AIDS was considered a "homosexual disease." Because of discrimination against gay men, the media ignored AIDS and few doctors wanted to research it. Soon, though, scientists discovered that anyone could get AIDS if HIV (human immunodeficiency virus) entered their bloodstream. In 1985, thirteen-year-old Ryan White contracted AIDS through a blood transfusion. At first, White faced fierce discrimination at school and in his community. White became a tireless AIDS activist and helped rally the public to fight AIDS. Salt-N-Pepa worked to educate the public about how condoms can protect people against HIV and AIDS. "Let's Talk About AIDS" raised public awareness of this issue.

as domestic violence, low-birth-weight babies, and inner-city violence. Pepa told former Supremes star Mary Wilson in *Interview* magazine that she felt a responsibility to her fans. She said, "People look up to us. Teenagers look up to us. We all have little sisters and cousins who look up to us, and we see what they go through. So we have to set an example . . . You have to give your fans and your children something that they can use in life."

INDEPENDENT

After *Blacks' Magic*, the ladies of Salt-N-Pepa faced many challenges. Given their success writing and producing, the women wanted more creative control over their own music. But there was a hitch: Azor felt like he had made the group. He got a very generous cut of all of Salt-N-Pepa's money. According to *Essence* magazine, Next Plateau Records paid Azor's production company $5 million in production costs over the years for Salt-N-Pepa's albums. The trio got half the money, which they had to split three ways. Azor got the other half. Azor also owns the names Salt, Pepa, and Spinderella. Even after parting ways with the group, he continued to profit financially from its success.

On top of all this, Salt and Azor were having personal problems. She felt that he was unwilling to commit to their relationship. She knew he was cheating on her, but she loved him so much that she didn't know what to do. She told writer Harry Allen, "Me and Hurby built the whole thing [Salt-N-Pepa] together. We were always together. We went to the studio together. We spent every waking moment together." One day Salt put her cards on the table. She asked Azor to marry her. He said no. Salt broke their relationship off for good.

Breaking up with Azor was one of the hardest things Salt ever did. Luckily, Pepa and Spinderella were there to help her through it. Salt moved in with Pepa in the summer of 1989, and the two began to rebuild their friendship, which had experienced harsh strain over the years. Salt fell into a deep

29

depression. The only thing that could save her from it was the birth of her first child, daughter Corinne. Cheryl told Harry Allen, "When Corinne came, it was just all about her!"

Although Salt's break with Azor was painful, it was ultimately good for her. It was also good for Salt-N-Pepa. The women were finally able to take a more active role in making their music and creating their own image. And they were brought closer together than ever.

MOTHERHOOD

By 1993, each member of Salt-N-Pepa had had her first child. At first, it was a bit traumatic as each member of the group found that her relationship didn't last long enough to provide her child with a full-time father. In other words, they all became single mothers. Luckily, they were able to help each other through pregnancies and child rearing. In fact, Salt was Pepa's Lamaze coach!

Motherhood changed each of the ladies for the better. Having children forced them to slow down and take a good look at their lives. The time for partying and being glamorous stars was over. Now they had to really focus on their families. They became more religious and focused on trying to make a real difference in the world. As Spinderella said in *Essence* magazine, "When you have a beautiful, precious baby, a new responsibility, you start to see things in a different light."

The members of Salt-N-Pepa dance and act in a video shoot for a track on their *Very Necessary* album at New York City's Club USA on August 30, 1993.

Three years had passed since Salt-N-Pepa released its last album. Many members of the press and the hip-hop community were ready to write off the group as a has-been.

VERY NECESSARY

Salt-N-Pepa surprised everyone by negotiating a new, more profitable record deal with London Records. In 1993, the group

Salt-N-Pepa give their acceptance speech at the thirty-seventh annual Grammy Awards on March 1, 1995, after winning the Grammy for Best Rap Performance by a Duo or Group for "None of Your Business."

returned to the studio to produce *Very Necessary*. Although Azor contributed some songs, the ladies took more initiative than ever on this album. For instance, both Salt and Pepa helped write "Shoop," which became one of their greatest hits.

Very Necessary gave Salt-N-Pepa a new sound and a new look. The videos featured a more grown-up Salt-N-Pepa in up-to-the-minute fashions, with plenty of dancing and sophisticated production values. No longer fly girls from the 'hood, the women of Salt-N-Pepa looked like they had just walked off designer runways. Smoother and infused with R & B, their sound was much more sophisticated. "Shoop" was a witty, laid-back song about one of Salt-N-Pepa's favorite topics: men. And "Whatta Man," a collaboration with popular R & B group En Vogue, was a celebration of finding a really good boyfriend. The song's soulful, catchy vocals, good-time lyrics, and excellent video made it one of their hottest singles. *Very Necessary* went multiplatinum, and in 1994, Salt-N-Pepa finally won a Grammy for Best Rap Performance by a Duo or Group, for the song "None of Your Business."

CHAPTER FOUR

NEW DIRECTIONS, THE FUTURE, AND INFLUENCES

Salt-N-Pepa followed up the immensely successful *Very Necessary* with a variety of new projects. The group contributed songs to soundtracks and to the compilation benefit album *Ain't Nothing But a She Thang*. Through a multimillion-dollar deal with MCA Records, they were able to begin their own record label, Jireh Records, in order to produce groups like Modern Yesterday, Day ta Day, and Eboni.

The ladies of Salt-N-Pepa had become entrepreneurs. They also tried their hands at expanding into other types of businesses. Spinderella opened up a

OTHER COMPILATIONS AND SOUNDTRACKS

Salt-N-Pepa has released a lot of music, and not all of it has been on the group's actual albums. The group also contributed to the compilation benefit album *Nothing But a She Thang* and to many soundtracks. Some of the soundtracks Salt-N-Pepa appear on are *10 Things I Hate About You*; *Space Jam*; *Juice*; *Prêt-à-Porter*; *Panther*; *To Wong Foo, Thanks for Everything! Julie Newmar*; and *Our Friend Martin*, a movie about Martin Luther King Jr.

beauty salon in Queens called She Things, and Pepa began an Atlanta clothing store named Hollyhood.

An interest in controlling their own financial destinies wasn't the only important new feature of the ladies' lives. All of the women had also rediscovered their Christian faith. Salt was particularly transformed by her deepened beliefs. Between her new religious zeal and her status as a mother, she began to feel uncomfortable with the racy content of Salt-N-Pepa's earlier albums. Around this time, Salt told writer Harry Allen, "I don't want to do 'Push It' no more, I don't want to 'Shoop' no more, I don't want to 'Gitty Up' no more. It's all fun for me right now, and I'm not bugging out. But I would like to turn the gospel circuit upside down; start doing some serious gospel rap music and corner that."

BRAND NEW

Meanwhile, Salt-N-Pepa continued to grow musically. The group worked harder than ever to produce *Brand New*, which was released in 1997, and featured Queen Latifah, Kirk Franklin, the Sounds of Blackness, Sheryl Crow, and other special guests. The album was more positive and political than ever but still included some old-fashioned party anthems. The ladies contributed to every song and took great pride in the album.

Salt *(left)*, Pepa *(center)*, and Spinderella link arms as they participate in a Stop the Violence march in Brooklyn, New York, on August 17, 1997.

Some critics felt that it was their best work yet. Unfortunately, *Brand New* produced disappointing sales.

LOVE AND FAMILY

On the personal front, the ladies were facing new changes and challenges. Salt finally found the love of her life in carpenter Gavin Wray, who joined her in producing tracks for *Brand New*. Later, Wray built a studio in the basement of their house, and the couple started a new record label called Gavfam.

Pepa and her husband Treach (of Naughty by Nature) pose for photographers backstage at the Source Awards in 1999.

In 1999, Pepa made her ten-year-long relationship with Treach of hip-hop group Naughty by Nature official in what some called the hip-hop wedding of the decade. It seemed like a match made in heaven. The couple met when they were both performing for an MTV Spring Break concert. Treach dared Pepa to bungee jump—and was shocked when she went through with it. The pair found that they had a lot in common. After a ten-year-long on-again-off-again relationship, the couple was married by Reverend Run of the pioneering hip-hop group Run DMC. Unfortunately, the couple divorced not long afterward. But they did have a child together, Egypt Jahnari, who became a little sister to Pepa's son, Tyran Moore.

PARTING WAYS

Eventually, as all members of the group began to move in different directions, Salt decided to leave the group. As she wrote in the book *Working Musicians:*

DISCOGRAPHY

Hot, Cool, and Vicious, Next Plateau (1986)
A Salt with a Deadly Pepa, London (1988)
A Blitz of Salt-N-Pepa Hits, London (1989)
Blacks' Magic, London/Next Plateau (1990)
Very Necessary, London (1993)
Brand New, London (1997)
The Best of Salt 'n Pepa, FFRR (2000)

Breaking up Salt-N-Pepa wasn't a mutual decision. I was the one who couldn't take it anymore. People were like "you know how much money you could make?" Salt-N-Pepa's a household name. Even on a failed album we were still in demand. I couldn't believe it. It was really hard for both of us but it was time to be individuals and have separate lives and do different things.

The wild ride that had been Salt-N-Pepa was finally over.

BEYOND SALT-N-PEPA

Salt-N-Pepa is no longer touring the world, recording albums, and living life in the fast lane. After Salt-N-Pepa, the ladies went on to separate projects and separate lives. Spinderella became

Spinderella takes control of the turntables as a guest celebrity DJ at an Academy Awards celebration dinner at the House of Blues in West Hollywood, California, on March 23, 2003.

a respected radio DJ with a nationally syndicated hip-hop show and a slot on one of LA's biggest radio stations. Pepa has been guest starring in movies and television shows. Salt went on to record a successful single with gospel rap group God's Property. And in 2001, she released a solo album entitled *Salt of the Earth*, full of inspirational and devotional raps. She also collaborated with Christopher "Play" Martin of Kid 'N Play to create a gospel rap musical called *Rise*.

LASTING INFLUENCES

Salt-N-Pepa has inspired a new generation of women in hip-hop. Today, there are more successful female artists in hip-hop than ever before. Rappers such as Foxy Brown and Eve have taken their cues from Salt-N-Pepa's sexy fashions, glamorous image, and no-nonsense attitudes. Missy "Misdemeanor" Elliot not only writes and produces her own songs, but she is also one of hip-hop's most respected, sought-after producers. And Grammy winner Lauryn Hill's lyrics, many of which encourage women and girls to respect themselves, echo Salt-N-Pepa's feminist and activist values. Each one of these women is making her mark in the still largely male-dominated world of hip-hop, while expressing herself and having fun. And that's what Salt-N-Pepa was always about.

Salt-N-Pepa has had a lasting and positive influence on hip-hop. It inspired many women to feel better about themselves and take control of their lives. The group has supported worthy causes concerning education on AIDS, domestic violence, low-birth-weight babies, and inner-city violence. And the members of the group have also managed to build satisfying home lives and successful careers. Everything the group has achieved was done through the power of friendship, hard work, belief in themselves, and service to others. As Salt told *Ebony* magazine in 1998:

> *I want people to say that Salt-N-Pepa gave back . . . they were real. They were true to themselves. They were the Harriet Tubmans of hip-hop. They made it, came back to get one and came back again to get another one.*

TIMELINE

1969   Sandra "Pepa" Denton is born in Kingston, Jamaica, on November 9. Cheryl "Salt" James is born in Brooklyn, New York, on March 28.

1971   Deirdre "Spinderella" Roper is born in New York City on August 3, 1971.

1985   Hurby "Luv Bug" Azor, Cheryl James, and Sandra Denton record "The Show Stopper (Is Stupid Fresh)." The new group calls itself Super Nature.

1986   Super Nature gets a record contract on Next Plateau Records. The group changes its name to Salt-N-Pepa and releases its first album *Hot, Cool, and Vicious.*

1987   Deirdre Roper replaces Pamela Latoya Greene as the group's Spinderella. "Push It" sells more than a million copies, tops R & B charts, and earns Salt-N-Pepa its first Grammy nomination for Best Rap Performance.

1988   Salt-N-Pepa releases *A Salt with a Deadly Pepa.*

1989   Salt-N-Pepa releases a remix album, *A Blitz of Salt-N-Pepa Hits.*

1990 Salt-N-Pepa releases *Blacks' Magic*. Cheryl, Sandra, and Dee Dee contribute creatively to several songs.

1992 At news anchor Peter Jennings's request, Salt-N-Pepa re-records its hit "Let's Talk About Sex" as "Let's Talk About AIDS." The video is featured on a television special about AIDS and becomes a public service announcement.

1993 Salt-N-Pepa releases *Very Necessary*, its biggest hit album yet. It features the songs "Shoop" and "Whatta Man."

1994 Salt-N-Pepa performs at the huge outdoor music festival Woodstock 1994.

1995 Salt-N-Pepa wins a Grammy for Best Rap Performance by a Duo or Group for "None of Your Business." A multimillion-dollar deal with MCA Records allows the women to create Jireh Records.

1997 Salt-N-Pepa releases its album *Brand New*, featuring guest artists Sheryl Crow, Kirk Franklin, and Queen Latifah.

2001 After the breakup of Salt-N-Pepa, Cheryl James's solo debut album, *Salt of the Earth*, is released.

GLOSSARY

Afrocentric Modeled on African cultures and traditions.

b-boy/b-girl People who identified themselves as part of the hip-hop culture in the developing years of hip-hop.

break The funkiest part of a record. This word is related to the term "breakdown."

DJ Disc jockey. The DJ mixes music together, traditionally on two turntables.

fly Beautiful and stylish.

freestyle An improvised rap created on the spot, often during a rhyming battle.

go-go A regional Washington, D.C., party music style, made by live bands with lots of percussion and horns.

hype Best, new, exciting, and/or fresh.

MC Master of ceremonies. This is an old-school term for "rapper."

old school Rap from the earliest days of hip-hop. Old school can also refer to the fashion style or trends of the late 1970s and early 1980s.

FOR MORE INFORMATION

Hip Hop Archive at the W. E. B. DuBois Institute for African and
African American Research
Harvard University
Barker Center
12 Quincy Street
Cambridge, MA 02138
(671) 496-6621
e-mail: info@hiphoparchive.org
Web site: http://www.hiphoparchive.org

Project Movement
132 West Fourth Street
New York, NY 10012
Web site: http://www.projectmovement.com

Web Sites

Due to the changing nature of Internet links, the Rosen Publishing
Group, Inc., has developed an online list of Web sites related to
the subject of this book. This site is updated regularly. Please use
this link to access the list:

http://www.rosenlinks.com/lhhb/sape

FOR FURTHER READING

Ayazi-Hashjin, Sherry. *Rap and Hip Hop: The Voice of a Generation.* New York, NY: Rosen Publishing, 1999.

Fricke, Jim, and Charlie Ahearn. *Yes Yes Y'all: The Experience Music Project Oral History of Hip-Hop's First Decade.* Cambridge, MA: Da Capo Press, 2002.

Gaar, Gillian. *She's a Rebel: The History of Women in Rock & Roll.* Seattle, WA: Seal Press, 1992.

Greenberg, Keith Elliot. *Rap.* Minneapolis, MN: Lerner Publications Company, 1988.

Hager, Steven. *Hip Hop: The Illustrated History of Break Dancing, Rap Music, and Graffiti.* New York, NY: St. Martin's Press, 1984.

Lomml, Cookie. *History of Rap Music.* Philadelphia, PA: Chelsea House Publishers, 2001.

Sexton, Adam, ed. *Rap on Rap.* New York, NY: Delta, 1995.

Vibe Magazine. *Hip Hop Divas.* New York, NY: Three Rivers Press, 2001.

BIBLIOGRAPHY

Allen, Harry. "The Queens from Queens." *Hip Hop Divas*. New York, NY: Three Rivers Press, 2001.

Chappell, Kevin. "The Salt-N-Pepa Nobody Knows—A Look at the Personal Lives of Cheryl James, Sandi Denton and Dee Dee Roper of the Music Group, Salt-N-Pepa." *Ebony*, Vol. 53, No. 4, February 1998.

Garr, Gillian. *She's a Rebel: The History of Women in Rock & Roll*. Seattle, WA: Seal Press, 1992.

Havelock, Nelson, and Michael A. Gonzalez. *Bring the Noise: A Guide to Rap Music and Hip-Hop Culture*. New York, NY: Harmony Books, 1991.

Keyes, Cheryl. *Rap Music and Street Consciousness*. Chicago, IL: University of Illinois Press, 2002.

Ogg, Alex, and David Upshal. *The Hip Hop Years: A History of Rap*. London, England: Channel 4 Books (MacMillan Publishers), 1999.

Pollock, Bruce, ed. *Working Musicians: Defining Moments from the Road, the Studio, and the Stage*. New York, NY: Harper Entertainment, 2002.

Rose, Tricia. *Black Noise: Rap Music and Black Culture in Contemporary America*. Hanover, NH: University Press of New England,1994.

INDEX

About the Author

Sahara Gisnash is a native of Oakland, California. She grew up listening to hip-hop, and loves Salt-N-Pepa. She now lives in Brooklyn, New York, where she writes books, radio scripts, and plays. She enjoys playing violin and traveling.

Photo Credits

Cover © Young Russell/Corbis Sygma; pp. 1, 25 © Getty Images, Inc.; p. 8 © Raymond Boyd/Michael Ochs Archives; p. 11 © New Line Cinema/courtesy Everett Collection; p. 13 © Johnny Nunez/ Wirelmage.com; pp. 17, 20 © Michael Ochs Archives; p. 27 © Al Pereira/Michael Ochs Archives; p. 31 © Steve Eichner/PhotoWeb/ Wirelmage.com; pp. 32, 35 © AP/Wide World Photos; p. 36 © Robert Hepler/Everett Collection; p. 38 © Mike Gusatella/ Wirelmage.com.

Designer: Thomas Forget; Editor: Wayne Anderson